THEATRE ROYAL MEMORIES

by

John Dixon

RB
Rossendale Books

Published by Rossendale Books

11 Mowgrain View, Bacup,
Rossendale, Lancashire
OL13 8EJ
England

http://www.rossendalebooks.co.uk

Published in paperback 2012

Category: Memoirs/Non-Fiction

ISBN: 978-1-906801-73-1

Contents

Acknowledgements

First of all I would like to thank the staff of the Theatre Royal, past and present, for their contributions in compiling this book. Special thanks must go to Chief Executive Philip Bernays, who supported my original concept and arranged unlimited access to the venue, as well as Marianne Quayle, Press and Communications Officer, who has supported the venture and made access to images and interviews possible (while no doubt tearing her hair out behind the scenes).

Also to Billy Clark, who supplied me with numerous stories and allowed me to tour back stage with him. Michael Harrison, Managing Director of Qdos Pantomimes, for taking the time and trouble to write the foreword and supply his own memories. Also for the access to his productions playing at the Theatre Royal and making the Theatre Royal pantomimes the best in the country. I know, like me, the Theatre Royal played an important part in his life as he grew up in the North East.

My wife Pam, and our daughters, Fern and Sian, who have given me the support, encouragement and opportunity to write this book. Also, for visiting many theatres with me while I am reviewing or just seeing a show for pleasure. Often I know they sit through shows they would not normally want to see, but it is appreciated, honest!

Finally to my late Grandfather, Albert Battman (of Hebburn), who started my relationship with the Theatre Royal.

Introduction

The Theatre Royal has always been part of my life since I attended my first pantomime in the early 1960s, and over the past few years I have been fortunate to review many shows at the venue. As well as reviewing for websites and the press, I receive invites to press launches and it was during one of these that I first had the idea for this project.

The press had been invited to the Olivier Suite, within the Theatre Royal, to hear about the forthcoming restoration, which would close the Theatre Royal for six months. We were given details of the forthcoming transformation, which would return the venue back to its original splendour, as Matcham had intended. While at the same time being able to cope with present day Health and Safety requirements and the demands of touring theatre productions for years to come. During the discussion on the new seating (which Susan Hampshire, who was appearing at the Theatre that week was more than happy to try out) I started to think back as to what my Grandfather would think, as he had been instrumental in introducing me to the Theatre Royal. Suddenly, memories started to flash through my head, many of which I had not thought about for years, if at all. This later set me thinking that if I had all these stories, other people must have similar memories and I approached Philip Bernays, Chief Executive of the Theatre Royal, with the idea of capturing people's memories. Philip was very supportive of the idea from the start and via interviews on the radio, telephone calls, face to face meetings, articles in the press, emails and letters, today we have a collection of memories associated with the Theatre Royal.

One of the stories involved being interviewed by the Evening Chronicle and to obtain a suitable photograph we were given access to the auditorium during the refurbishment. This allowed me to see the work going on at close hand and the opportunity to stand up against the very ceiling of the auditorium, where the chandelier had been. Since the Theatre Royal reopened I often look up at the roof, remembering standing up there alongside the gold leaf, an opportunity few people have had.

It was never my intention to have a chronological listing of productions which have played the Theatre Royal, but to put together a selection of people's memories from when they visited the Theatre Royal or other events associated to the venue. However, along the way, we will of course reflect on the productions and actors who have appeared on the Theatre Royal stage. Several performers have contributed their own memories and at the end is a "meander through the decades" of a selection of productions, which have played the Theatre Royal.

But it is worth remembering that this collection has been made up of people's memories, some going back many years, so time could have played a part in adjusting the truth and they may have become embellished with each retelling, but no doubt they are all based on fact.

When I commenced this project I wondered if people would respond. But I realised that I was not alone in having special memories of the Theatre Royal when Mrs. J. Dinning of Gosforth wrote to me, closing her letter, which related to meeting Dickie Valentine, with the words:
"Thank you for giving me the opportunity to re-live my happy memory of the Theatre Royal".

That one letter made this whole project worthwhile.

Foreword

The Theatre Royal Newcastle - loved and adored by thousands of people, some of whom have contributed here to John Dixon's excellent collection of stories and memories from the people who make the Theatre Royal what it is - a "magic" place.

People care about the Theatre Royal. Audiences have obviously witnessed great productions there over the years but there are those who have fallen in love, courted, spent precious moments with loved ones, and, importantly, introduced their children and grand children to theatre there to say nothing of the many performers who have appeared on its famous stage.

The grand old Lady of Grey Street has entertained hundreds of thousands of theatre-goers from the North East and beyond. During her 175 years there have been so many wonderful productions presented at the theatre so here's to the next 175 years of "magic" at the Theatre Royal.

Michael Harrison
Managing Director of Qdos Pantomimes
January 2012

Running Themes

Out of all the people who have contacted me with their memories, there seems to be one area that many of them remember all too well, myself included, "The Gods". This area of the Theatre Royal is a one we will return to several times during our trip down memory lane.

Although the seats in the Gallery and now the Amphitheatre (first few rows of the Gallery) are now able to be booked, this has not always been the case. I took the picture shown here just before the 2011 refurbishment, which shows the seats fitted in the 1980's refit. I always used to, and still do, call this area of the Theatre Royal, "The Gods"; I know many people of my generation still

do. The entrance for The Gods was in Shakespeare Street and the audience used to queue up the side of the Theatre Royal and even round on to Pilgrim Street, waiting for the dedicated box office to open. There was no pre-booking, just turn up, hand over your money and get the best seat you could. At the allocated time a large door was swung open to reveal a small box office, where a cashier was sitting behind a grille, ready to sell tickets on a first come, first served, basis. Once you had paid for your tickets, the race was on to climb those stone steps as quickly as you could to secure the best seat in the house. At one time the seating was just wooden benches, but I recall in the late 1960's there was padding, but no backs.

I have not watched a show from this area of the Theatre Royal for many years, but recall it was always one particular Great Aunt, who took me to see shows on a Saturday afternoon, sitting in The Gods. When I visited with my Grandfather, we always sat in the stalls, as his health would not have allowed him to climb all the way to the top and in those days there was no lift. The heat was often unbearable up there and the view, due to the height, meant you could see behind some of the sets and had to watch the top of the heads of a lot of the performers. Joe Pasquale in part of his act lies down on stage so the people in The Gods can see what he looks like.

I can recall during one pantomime in the late 1960's, ***Aladdin*** I seem to recall, (when a character was rolled between two large rollers and then emerged again as a flat cardboard cut out) from The Gods you could see the actor being helped through the rollers by the stage hands and the cut out being slid in to place. This would have been invisible to the rest of the audience; it was the height of The Gods which gave it away. Whenever that scene is included in any pantomime today, it always makes me remember The Gods of the Theatre Royal.

If you are used to sitting in the Stalls or Grand Circle you should visit this area of the Theatre, either at the interval or try watching a production from up

there. It does not seem that far when looking up from the stage or stalls, but try looking down, it gives a whole different perspective. Paul Nicholas in ***Barnum*** and Danny Adams in a recent pantomime, both launched themselves off this area of the Theatre Royal to descend across people's heads while clinging on to a rope in zip wire fashion. I followed Danny on one occasion, when writing an article about being backstage during the performance, and while I was out of breath by the time I got to the Gallery, Danny had to do the same climb, mid way through a performance, twice a day for several weeks. He literally came off stage, and ran up the stairs to The Gods, where stage crew made sure he was safely secured, before he stepped off the ledge and flew past the audience in the Upper and Grand Circles, skimmed the heads of those in the stalls, and ended back on stage to close the first half of the pantomime. Needless to say, I was still getting my breath back by the interval and then faced taking the stairs back down!

Likewise, people recall the venue before the 1980's refit, when there was a separate entrance for the Upper Circle in the main foyer. From the foyer you turned left and took a direct staircase to the Upper Circle, the Grand Circle was to the right. But after the stairway was out of sight of the foyer, the fittings that matched the rest of the main entrance stopped and it became a much more basic affair, identifying you as being segregated from the more expensive areas of the venue. Today there is no such segregation, as everyone enters via the main entrance.

When I first started to visit the Theatre there was a coffee bar at the back of the Grand Circle which had large glass windows, looking in to the auditorium. I recall coffee was served in large glass, Pyrex type cups with matching saucers. But when sitting in the Grand Circle, you could often hear the clatter of the cups being cleared up as the show started after the interval. The picture above not only shows the glass windows at the back of the Grand Circle but the centre aisles which were present until the 1980's refit.

I do recall sitting in the Upper Circle when Pat Phoenix and Alan Browning (both from Coronation Street at the time) starred in a production of ***Gaslight*** many years ago. We left the Upper Circle to have a drink in the coffee bar at the back of the Grand Circle, which could only be accessed via the foyer. So each way, it was a trip all the way down, across the foyer and then back up. For the return journey, for reasons that escape me, we left it too late and it is the only time I can ever remember entering a theatre after the performance has started.

It has taken a long time to find someone who actually remembered this Grand Circle coffee bar, as I had started to wonder if it was a figment of my imagination, but thanks to Billy Clark, who we will hear more of later, I have had my memories confirmed!

The building itself has been altered over the years. The stairs to the right when you walk in that lead to the Grand Circle were originally closed in. Now you can look through to the Grand Circle Bar as you climb the stairs and there are doors straight ahead to allow access to the Grand Circle.

But even the foyer has changed, I can recall the small ticket booth selling returns or unsold tickets from within the foyer, (just visible on the left of the picture above) but this area as we know it today used to be a lot smaller, with the box office being down one side. However, the general look and feel of the foyer remains the same, even though today the audience can gain access to any part of the Theatre Royal from here as well as walk through to a restaurant and book tickets.

In this picture you can see the same stairs behind my children in February 2008, during the long run of the musical CATS. My wife runs a face painting business called ***Fun For Faces*** and face painted during the run, with her stand being located at the bottom of the stairs.

On a Saturday the queue from the matinee performance for face painting sometimes was still in place as the evening audiences started to arrive! It is hard to imagine all the changes that have happened around those stairs over the years. What would the audiences of the past decades make of that, I wonder?

A Royal Autumn Evening

Several members of the Royal Family have visited the Theatre Royal over the years. But Sunday October 14th 1990 was very special, as there was a Royal Gala Performance, attended by Their Royal Highnesses The Duke and Duchess of York. The evening was in aid of The Dene Centre and Calvert Trust, Kielder.

In the week preceding, ***Time and the Conways*** played at the Theatre Royal. The J. B. Priestley play provides a time slip where after seeing a family gather for a twenty first birthday celebration, we watch the future, while being powerless to change the course of events. This production was special as it starred Joan Plowright, the widow of Laurence Olivier. She was joined on stage by Tamsin Olivier and Julie Kate Olivier, with Richard Olivier directing.

The Royal Gala itself starred Rebecca Storm, who had appeared in many West End musicals. She was accompanied by Chris Corcoran, who was no stranger to musicals at the Theatre Royal and boxing legend Frank Bruno. I recall the evening was beset by sound problems, at the time blamed on outside radio frequencies. But there was not a spare seat in the auditorium. Ticket prices included a donation to the aforementioned charities and ranged from £100 in the Grand Circle to £10 in the Gallery.

I had only seen ***Time and the Conways*** the previous evening, so the transformation of the now "Royal Box" resplendent in flowers went some way to demonstrate the work that had gone on inside the Theatre Royal during the last twenty four hours. To complete the weekend, I booked to see John Inman in ***Pyjama Tops*** the following night. The "hilarious romp" opened on the Monday night after the Gala, for a one week run. While Inman did mention the Royal Gala during the performance, the comedy was poorly attended and not the non-stop laughter riot promised. After seeing a spellbinding play on the Saturday and the Royal Gala on the Sunday, here we were back to earth with a bump on the Monday.

Theatre Ghost

While many stories of the Theatre Royal Ghost exist, Billy Clark and Ray Irwin, past and present stage doorkeepers at the Theatre Royal have vivid memories of their own separate encounters with the Ghost. Interestingly both state there was no shape of a human, but a mist or cloud. However, there are the other stories; one of the usherettes approaching a man sitting smoking in the Stalls, pointed out he was not allowed to smoke and turned away, but upon turning back to him, he had gone and there was not enough time for him to have reached any of the exits; one of the backstage crew opened the male toilets to find a lady putting make-up on, he immediately apologised and went back outside. To confirm he had not made a mistake he reopened the toilet door to find no one there.

Ray Irwin, Stage Doorkeeper, tells me that he was working overnight one Sunday, when he started to hear noises and briefly thought someone was locked in the venue following a production earlier that day. But upon checking, no one was there. Suddenly in the passage between the end of the stage and the green room, which passes the Stage Doorkeepers Office, a "mass" came swirling down the corridor. Ray telephoned a colleague about this and he just laughed "You've seen the ghost" came the reply.

It took a while before Ray would venture out of his office again that night.

Billy had a different encounter with the swirling mist. On one occasion when putting the Theatre Royal seats back (as they are removed to accommodate large orchestras) the permanent staff were still working around 2 a.m. Suddenly they were aware of a mist drifting across the Grand Circle. On another occasion, they ran out of screws, so Billy walked across to the prop room to get some more. Then he became aware of what sounded like a basket being dragged across the floor above, but there was no one else around. He checked with fellow stage crew and no one was on the landing above at the time.

During the War there had to be night watchmen at the Theatre Royal and one of these had an Alsatian dog. But when they went past the Assistant Manager's Office and entrance to the Amphitheatre the dog would always turn sideways and pull away from the door, but the office was empty…

My Memories

I have a lot of memories over the past fifty or so years regarding the Theatre Royal and thought it only fair to share many of these, while remaining conscious that this project is not just about my recollections and stories.

The 1960's are where my memories of the Theatre Royal start, the first being the family annual outing to the pantomime. The tradition had been to always attend on Boxing Day, until one year the building was apparently extremely cold and the elderly relatives claimed it had given them colds and flu. Hence the Boxing Day panto outing became a thing of the past, just as I was old enough to go!

However, a few years later I started to attend the Theatre Royal regularly with my maternal Grandfather and a maiden Aunt of my Father. This allowed me to appreciate the difference between sitting in the Stalls to The Gods.

Although I have never objected to The Gods, as it meant a trip to the Theatre. However sitting in the front stalls on a Saturday night with my Grandfather was my preferred option, not that I was ever given a choice anyway.

The routine was almost set in stone: I would stay with my parents as they worked at the family business (A. Battman and Partners in Hebburn), named after my Grandfather, Albert Battman, who lived in Tharsis Road, Hebburn. You can imagine the problems when the TV caped crusader shows started! Each year a new set of school children thought it was fun to hold open the shop door and scream the signature tune! It never occurred to them the spelling was different.

Above he is pictured with me on what appears to be a family holiday at Butlins.

After the office closed on a Saturday afternoon, I would go to his house for tea before driving to Newcastle in his green Triumph 2000 automatic. I can still recall the black interior that was kept in pristine condition, there was never any mess or anything allowed in that could spill. We would park in Dex car park, behind what was then the Odeon Cinema, and walk over to the Theatre Royal. Adverts for the Dex Garage used to appear in the Theatre Royal programme. The garage, unlike the Odeon, is still operating from the same site, but now run by a national company, however the name Dex can clearly be seen in the brickwork. I am sure you could have your car valet cleaned when you left your vehicle, and you also gave in your keys so the car was parked by the attendants.

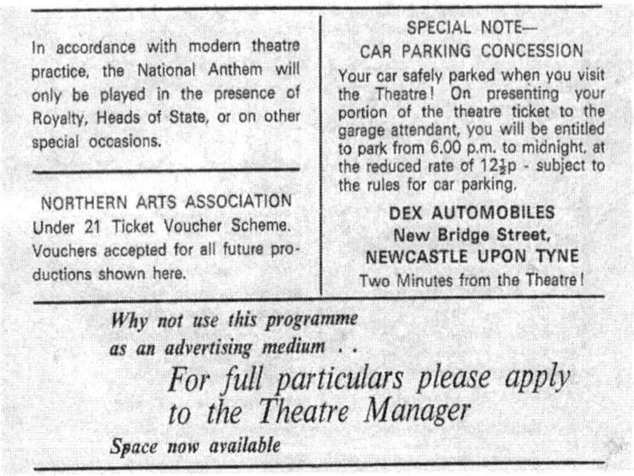
In accordance with modern theatre practice, the National Anthem will only be played in the presence of Royalty, Heads of State, or on other special occasions.

NORTHERN ARTS ASSOCIATION
Under 21 Ticket Voucher Scheme. Vouchers accepted for all future productions shown here.

SPECIAL NOTE—
CAR PARKING CONCESSION
Your car safely parked when you visit the Theatre! On presenting your portion of the theatre ticket to the garage attendant, you will be entitled to park from 6.00 p.m. to midnight, at the reduced rate of 12½p - subject to the rules for car parking.

DEX AUTOMOBILES
New Bridge Street,
NEWCASTLE UPON TYNE
Two Minutes from the Theatre!

Why not use this programme as an advertising medium . .
For full particulars please apply to the Theatre Manager
Space now available

After the performance we returned to his house, where I slept in his front bedroom under what was the heaviest eiderdown (no duvets in those days).

We seemed to repeat this week after week, but looking back at the productions when researching these memories, I realised they were spaced out. However, the listings identify many shows I wish we had seen. Perhaps my age at the time made it unlikely I would sit through certain productions, but I can never recall being told to either pay attention or sit still, nor was I guilty of numerous trips to the toilet, which seem to grip many young children when they visit the theatre or cinema and lose interest.

I also recall being determined to be one of the children on stage at the end of the pantomime! It took three attempts one year to do it, but finally I lined up, did whatever was asked of me and got a prize. I seem to remember it was an animal made of balloons. On that memorable day I made it on to the stage, I was with another Great Aunt and we turned up for a matinee to see if any tickets might be on sale. These returns or late sales were made from the small kiosk in the middle of the foyer. I do recall we got the tickets but they were not together. My Aunt had to sit in the Grand Circle and I was at the side of the front stalls. I am not sure how I convinced her to allow me to sit alone, as I was obviously still young, but I proudly took my prize home on the bus.

There is little doubt I have inherited my love of live shows from my Grandfather. He used to spend many family summer holidays at Blackpool, (there were no trips to Spain in his day). Many top acts played for weeks on end during the summer season, in a variety of theatres, which littered the town. I can remember him telling me he used to take in two shows a day, racing between venues. Years later I have done the same but this time in London's West End. I can instantly recall packing my Mother in to a taxi after a matinee of ***"Underneath the Arches"*** to ensure we reached the Vaudeville Theatre in time for the farce ***"Key for Two"*** (it was so tight for timing we could not take our coats off until the interval as we arrived as the lights were dimming). While a friend and I used to spend many long weekends in London, we always had trouble filling in the mornings before the matinees.

This year will see me heading for around my thirtieth Royal Variety Performance, with our daughters having started to attend with my wife and I, four years ago. I wonder what my Grandfather would make of that? In his lifetime he would never have dreamt regular members of the public would be able to attend such a prestigious show.

The last time we went to the Theatre Royal together was to see ***Boeing Boeing***, starring several of the ***Man About The House*** cast, which was a massive TV hit at the time. I recall the Saturday evening was sold out, so I spent quite some time in the Box Office, waiting to see if there were any returns. Finally my wait paid off. The Box Office was at that time situated to the right of the main doors with a separate entrance. Since then it has moved from that location and back again. During the refurbishment in the 1980's the Box Office moved to the back of the building, facing the old fire station, then to inside the foyer. At the time of ***Boeing Boeing*** there were no computers, just rows of pigeonhole shelving, each containing books of tickets.

From a story you will read about later regarding an early tour of ***No! No! Nanette***, I recall a much later tour of the musical, which started life with Noelle Gordon (Crossroads) as the star. Sadly Ms. Gordon became very ill and Moira Lister headed the tour. Having booked to take my paternal Grandmother, Dorothy 'Dora' Dixon of Cresswell Road, Wallsend (pictured here) to see the show, we expected nothing untoward to happen as we sat in row F of the stalls (Row F in those days had a lot more leg room than other rows I seem to recall and there was still a central aisle). During the performance a man a few rows in front, visible to the cast on stage, stood up and was helped along the row where he collapsed under one of the boxes. I can still visualise him being taken out by an ambulance crew, as the cast on stage continued to high kick their way through another dance routine.

My Grandmother would come to the Theatre Royal for pantos and occasionally for other shows, but there always seemed to be an incident of some sort when she was there. During one of the pantos, we had front row stall seats (this is where we moved to after the Boxing Day visits stopped) and I recall the Dame made her entrance via the stalls and came along the front row, carrying a basket. For whatever reason, it could have been coats on the floor, Grandmother's legs, her stick, I do not know, but the Dame tripped and landed on top of her. I am not sure who got the bigger surprise! She claimed not to be hurt although her hat had a large dent in it, which she had to sort out, and she appeared to be uncomfortable for the rest of the show. However, we noticed the Dame was watching us during most of his scenes and he asked if she was ok from the stage on more than one occasion, including the finale.

On another visit we were watching ***Murder at the Vicarage*** and she fell asleep (many of us are guilty of that at times), but awoke with a start when the on stage gun was fired! Then after visiting Fenwick's in Northumberland Street for a meal I remember we went to a matinee of a ***Olde Time Musical Hall***, sadly the audience was few and far between. Although I can recall little of the acts, I do have recollections of us being asked to actually applaud!

However, the best memory related to the Theatre Royal concerning my Grandmother was taking her to see ***My Fair Lady***, starring Tony Britton, Liz Robertson and Dame Anna Neagle. Dame Anna had been one of Britain's biggest stars during the war and married film producer Herbert Wilcox. At the time I was working for Turners Film Productions. Turners used to have camera shops all over the North East and this was a specialist section, which made documentary films and worked on television programmes. This was long before video was around. One of the secretaries knew one of the stage doorkeepers at the time and arranged for me to meet Dame Anna after the matinee. I kept the visit secret, quizzing my Grandmother on what she knew about Dame Anna, worryingly she seemed to know all about the parts of her life which I thought were better not mentioned when we met!

After the matinee as we walked past the Stage Door, I suddenly opened it and asked my Grandmother to follow, which she did, surprisingly without asking why. We were told we were expected and had to go through another set of double doors and turn right, then knock on the first dressing room door, which I did. At that moment I turned back to see my Grandmother looking a bit shell shocked and pulling one of her signature hats in to place (she never went anywhere without a hat, but always altered the design slightly so it was unique, something she had done since her days as a milliner).

Dame Anna opened the door looked at me, smiled and asked immediately where my Grandmother was, before walking up the corridor to meet her. My Grandmother appeared to be rooted to the spot, but Dame Anna took her hand and led her in to the dressing room. We spent the next few minutes seeing the dresses Dame Anna had worn in the show before leaving, as she had the Matron from the Cheshire Homes waiting to see her. I then walked

Grandmother to Croft Street (opposite the old BBC Studios) where she caught the bus home to Wallsend and for the only time in my life I recall she was speechless. The story does not stop there though, as a short time after two boys pushed my Grandmother over in the street. We never knew who they were, just that she was walking home from her sister's a short distance from her house, when the boys approached laughing and deliberately knocked in to her. Sadly this was enough to make her fall and they left her lying in the gutter, unable to get up as they ran off. Nothing was stolen, but she sat at home unwilling to tell anyone about the incident for several days. From that time on we noticed a change in her personality and in her overall health, which we believe this incident triggered. However, Dame Anna took the time and trouble to send my Grandmother a Christmas card once she became aware of the incident.

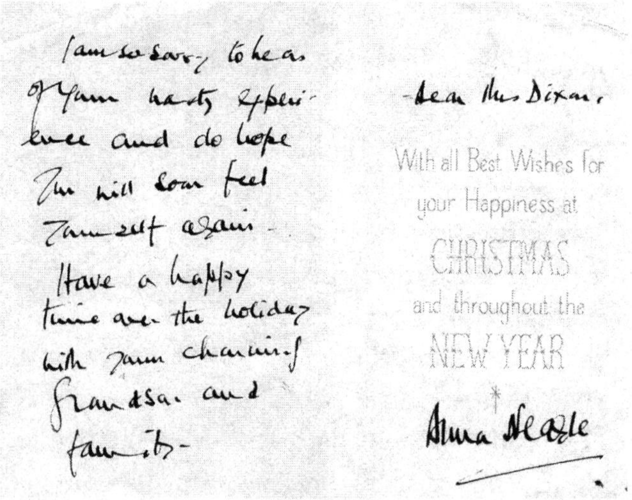
I am so sorry to hear
of your nasty experi-
ence and do hope
you will soon feel
yourself again.
Have a happy
time over the holiday
with your charming
grandson and
family.

Dear Mrs Dixon,
With all Best Wishes for
your Happiness at
CHRISTMAS
and throughout the
NEW YEAR
Anna Neagle

During my time at Turners I worked on 16 mm film documentaries and often we were hired out to the B.B.C. as a freelance film crew. On one such occasion we had to go to the Gosforth Park Hotel, where Sir Ralph Richardson was to be interviewed, as he was appearing at the Theatre Royal, in a play called **Early Days**. As we unpacked the car in the hotel car park, we spotted Sir Ralph watching us from his room, once he realised we had seen him, he acknowledged us with a wave. Everything was set up waiting for the great man to enter the interview room and you could sense the director's nervousness. But typical of a true star, when he arrived and later left the room, he personally shook hands with all the crew and thanked them for being there. To work so closely to such a great actor, let alone shake hands with him, was a tremendous experience, and built up my excitement for seeing the play. Sadly, when I did see it the next evening I recall being bitterly disappointed, although to see Sir Ralph perform on stage more than made up for it. But admittedly, it was one of those rare occasions when I did ask for an autograph (I had even travelled to the Theatre Royal the evening before the interview to buy a programme).

In my twenties I started my own photography business, but enjoyed the portrait side much more

than weddings, which were the real bread and butter work. I rented a display window next to Forest Hall flyover and regularly changed the photos. To try and catch people's attention I tried to mailshot visiting celebrities asking if I could take their picture. Usually I received a polite rejection, but both Norman Wisdom and Roy Hudd agreed. I photographed Norman Wisdom at the long gone, High Pitt Club in Cramlington, where he was appearing in cabaret. Roy Hudd was touring in a comedy playing at the Theatre Royal for one week. He asked me to meet him at the Theatre Royal and he duly arrived, having been watching snooker at his hotel. While I photographed him, he told me about appearing with Ethel Merman at the Royal Variety Performance and many other stories about the people he had worked with. Afterwards I sent him prints as a thank you and he returned one signed (pictured above). Afterwards he even placed an order.

My memories will hopefully continue to grow in years to come. But to bring the present collection to a close I have become one of Theatre Royal 175 Patrons, to support the recent refurbishment. Part of this included having your name on a seat, so I included the name of my wife and our daughters on the plaque. But I never told them. When we were invited to view the auditorium my wife and daughters thought our invite was either because of

this project, or due to the fact I review at the Theatre Royal. It was only during the speeches held on stage, with the curtain lowered, that they became aware that their names were on a seat in the Grand Circle (all the invited guests had entered via the Stage Door to keep the auditorium hidden until it was revealed in all its splendour, see picture below). During the

1980's refit my Mother had donated to the Theatre Royal and arranged for my name to be placed on the last seat of the front row in the Grand Circle seat, where I sat most Saturdays. The original plaque was replaced in the 2011 refit.

It is pure coincidence that our eldest daughter shares her birthday with the Theatre Royal! (Different years of course, there is a 163 year age gap.)

Memories from Actors & Theatre Royal Staff (Past and Present)

In 1977, the Royal Shakespeare Company made the first of what was to become their annual seasons at the Theatre Royal and **Dame Judi Dench recalls:**

"It was the first season that the RSC went to Newcastle and it was glorious without the strain of Stratford. It was a beautiful theatre and the audiences were so enthusiastic and warm and welcoming.

On the last night of the Comedy of Errors, the audience was encouraged to come up on stage to do the last song and dance. They were enjoying themselves so much that they did not want to leave, and we had to ask them to go.

Michael and Finty were with me and Finty was tiny so a good friend, Julie Churcher, came with us to look after her. One time they all went to Cullercoats to fly kites, but I could not go because I had a matinee. We stayed on a clifftop in Tynemouth and one day we could not get out of the house because it was so windy that we could not open the door.

I did lots of shopping and bought some boots in Fenwick's, which I loved so much that I wore them until they fell off my feet. I also had my ears pierced. However, the main memory is the warmth and enthusiasm of the audiences. I shall never forget it."

Several people have recalled what they describe as the definitive Peter Pan, when Bonnie Langford soared high across the stage doing cartwheels in the musical version of the show.

Bonnie contacted me from New York to supply her memories of this production:
"I was delighted to see that you are compiling a collection of memories about the Theatre Royal, Newcastle. It is quite some time since I have played there, however, it is still a beautiful and prestigious venue. Here are some thoughts for you ...... The Theatre Royal, Newcastle is such a noble theatre to play. I remember flying high as Peter Pan and feeling the spirit of 'performers past' almost literally in the air!

It is hard to describe the effect that history can play in our lives, but when you enter a theatre that has housed artists and audiences for many years, the echo of distant laughter and applause is almost tangible. The Theatre Royal was our last venue on a long and successful National tour of Peter Pan-The Musical and it was the perfect place to complete such a special production. It added a magical quality and sparkle to our adventures in Never, Neverland.!

Many happy returns to a beautiful, prestigious and majestic theatre. May it gloriously accommodate audiences and artists for countless generations."

Sir David Jason also recalls the Theatre Royal audiences as *"warm and welcoming"* when he played Buttons in Cinderella, opposite North East performers Leah Bell as Cinderella and Bobby

Thompson (who was the cabaret at Prince Charming's the Ball).

However, **Leah Bell** (who has appeared in two pantomimes at the Theatre Royal) shared another memory of this production with me. She recalls David Jason (in his first and only pantomime to date) used to feel sorry for an old man who turned up in a jumper and appeared to shuffle around during rehearsals. It was not until the show opened that David Jason had any idea how much the North East audiences loved Bobby Thompson and how big a star he was in the region. It then became apparent that David had felt so sorry for the "old man" during rehearsals that he had been slipping him money for a cup of tea and the bus fare home! At the time Bobby had his own Rolls Royce and was appearing at the Theatre Royal before going on to cabaret at the Mayfair over the Christmas period.

Ironically, in 2012 The Bobby Thompson Story will play the Theatre Royal.

Philip Bernays, Chief Executive of the Theatre Royal recalls:
"At my interview for the job of Chief Executive the Board, knowing that I had been a student at Newcastle University some 25 years previously asked, how often I had come to the Theatre Royal then. Never, I replied, as a student more interested in radical theatre I wouldn't have been seen dead here! Actually not quite true – I was stage crew on the RSC 1980 season in the then Gulbenkian Studio, and helped carry some props down from the Gulbenkian to the Theatre Royal for a rehearsal of Nicholas Nickleby. I carried them onto the stage and looked out into the auditorium – and thought it was a bit dark and oppressive (well I was a radical student – and the lights were probably turned off!)."

North East born **Michael Harrison**, Managing Director of Qdos Pantomimes, who has written, directed and produced the last seven smash hit pantomimes at the Theatre Royal tells me that:

"The Theatre Royal holds a special place in my heart. I love the place. I'm at home in the building. As a boy I would see the pantomime at the Royal sometimes up to 15 times a season. I fell in love with the magic of it all.

I dreamt of working at the Royal, of being part of the building and of course part of the pantomime - little did I know that some years later I would produce, write and direct at the time of writing, 7 Theatre Royal pantomimes.

I remember the excitement of arriving in the theatre, waiting for the show to start. I used to love (and still do) being the first person in the empty auditorium and watching it fill up to a packed house. Despite its seating capacity you feel very close to the stage which makes it perfect for pantomime. I love the fact that many audience members leave the panto at the end and then immediately re book for the following year. That's amazing satisfaction."

Billy Clark (performer and Stage Doorkeeper at the Theatre Royal) recalls on one occasion Laurence Olivier arrived at the Stage Door asking for Rex Harrison. The on duty Stage Doorkeeper asked who he should say was calling! Olivier had arrived at the Theatre Royal to ask Rex Harrison, in rehearsals for a play entitled ***August for the People***, to leave the production, so he could join the cast of Cleopatra.

The star of Cleopatra, Elizabeth Taylor, then visited the Theatre Royal to see Rex Harrison. She was joined by Richard Burton, both arriving in separate Rolls Royces at the Stage Door. Burton himself had played the Theatre Royal in May 1954, with The Old Vic Company, performing Hamlet and Twelfth Night. His co-stars were Fay Compton, Claire Bloom and Michael Horden.

Billy also remembers many years before Bonnie Langford played Peter Pan, Alastair Sim appeared as Captain Hook in a different version of the show. Hidden in the wings were a series of ladders, each boy had a stage hand ready to counter balance their attached wire so they could "fly" across the stage. During one of the performances, a " Lost Boy" mis-timed his cue, jumping off his ladder before his corresponding stagehand had a chance to counter balance the wire. This resulted in the actor flying in to the scenery and crashing to the stage, knocking himself out. Which in itself was bad enough, but as he launched himself off, the other "Lost Boys" all thought they had missed their cues and hurled themselves off their ladders. This resulted in "Lost Boys" flying everywhere, with arms and legs flaying in the air as stage hands tried to stop them crashing to the floor.

Over the years Billy has built up a wealth of stories, from his time performing with Albert Burdon, right through to being Stage Doorkeeper at the Theatre Royal. Recollections include forming friendships with many visiting performers who appeared at the Theatre Royal over the years and he has very fond memories of the likes of Linda Lusardi, who he ended up dancing with at a night club. When you realise he trained as a jockey you can understand what the pairing would have looked like. He appeared in pantomime at the Theatre Royal with Albert Burdon, after Burdon approached him when he saw his picture in a newspaper and wrote to him.

Billy worked at the Theatre Royal with his brothers back stage before becoming Stage Doorkeeper and has recollections of the "iron" which is known to the audience as the safety curtain, being pulled up by hand, as well as jumping off the fly wall, thirty-eight feet up - no health and safety worries in those days! In Billy's day he often used to work from Sunday right through to opening on a Monday night during a get in, with many stage crew working for the dairies, so with the early starts they were free for matinees.

During one pantomime the ***"Genie of the Lamp"*** the actor playing the Genie kept wanting to go higher when making his entrance through a trap door. Each time they tried the "Genie" wanted to go higher still, until finally extra weights were added by the stagehands to ensure that the Genie's wishes came true! Suddenly the Genie shot through the trap door in to the air, shouting "Not that high!" as he rose above the stage.

When a circus played at the Theatre Royal in the early 1950's Billy recalled that an elephant called Baby was appearing and it had to come through the scenery doors. The stage was re-enforced, as there were two elephants, lamas and ponies as well as a tank with two seals. Scaffolding was erected by the scenery door for Baby to enter; when the ringmaster arrived he asked what the scaffolding was for. When he was told it was for Baby he said half the size would do. So the scaffolding was changed. Then the elephant arrived and his keeper, Jock from Glasgow, left Baby standing by the dock doors as he came to see what was going on and again questioned the scaffolding. When he explained it was not needed the air turned slightly blue as the scaffolder took the rigging he had already altered away. Jock then shouted for Baby and the elephant wandered in through the dock doors stepping down on the floor of the wings, without the need for the scaffolding.

Billy also remembers forty dogs accompanied one act that took over Dressing Room 16. The dogs traveled with their owner in a bus and had to be taken upstairs in boxes, while the small dogs were transported in washing up bowls.

Flora Robson, in the days before she was a Dame appeared at the Theatre Royal and Billy recalls her as a "smashing lass". Billy had to prepare a meal for her during each performance. She would leave the stage, collect the meal and return on stage with it. As she exited the stage she would say to Billy "What have you got for me tonight Geordie?" He would answer "panackerty or whatever he had, and Flora answered "Oh lovely" before walking back on stage with the prepared meal.

During the run it was her birthday and she supplied beer and cigarettes (as in those days everyone smoked) for the crew. She then joined them in the prop room for a drink and when the Company Manager came looking for her (as there was a private function being held for her in the Grand Circle) she replied "It's my birthday and I am spending it with the lads". After a while he came back again and reluctantly Flora left the crew to join the party.

On another memorable occasion ***Goldilocks and the Three Bears*** was appearing at the Theatre Royal and Baby Bear took ill. As Billy was the only person who fitted the costume he took over the role until the actor recovered!

In the 1950s Tony Britton starred as Professor Higgins in ***My Fair Lady*** (a role he would reprise years later, when Dame Anna Neagle toured with him). There was an immediate bond between Billy and Tony Britton, which allowed Billy to shout "Rex Harrison" (who first played Higgins on stage as well as in the film version) at Britton whenever the opportunity arose (i.e., when the No. 1 dressing room door was left open or seeing each other outside). Britton always replied colourfully, with "off" invariably being the second word.

Years later their paths crossed again, Britton, immaculate as always, was walking in front of Billy, when he shouted "Mr. Britton" without turning around Britton replied "Yes" and Billy replied "Rex Harrison". We need not bother ourselves with the reply. Billy has encountered a lot of performers over the years including Laurence Olivier who performed as Othello, having his assistant polish him with velvet, so the black dye went in to his pores. But there were no private bathrooms in those days after the performance; a tin bath took pride of place in dressing room one, as Olivier scrubbed off the dye.

During another production there was a blackout allowing for a scene change, Billy raced over to the bed on stage and in the dark, grabbed a leg. He knew instantly by the hair it did not belong to Billy Whitelaw, who was also on stage, but to Laurence Olivier.

Olivier used to have people arrive ahead of him to check the equipment at theatres he was due to play. On one occasion they came to Billy and asked about his "thunder sheet" but upon examination was told, "Larry will not like that". Then he was asked about his rain effect, upon telling them it was a garden sieve with peas was told again "Larry will not like that". Finally he was asked "What about your wind machine? "I know" replied Billy, "Larry will not like that."

Dickie Valentine while appearing at the Theatre Royal received a letter from a girl who suffered from depression explaining to him that his records were the only thing that lifted her depression. She was invited backstage, no press were made aware and the meeting was kept low profile. Arrangements were made for Billy to get afternoon tea from the Turks Head Hotel, which was opposite the Theatre Royal, and have it set out in the dressing room. After the show the girl came backstage and spent time with Dickie, leaving before the second show began. "You know Billy, you make a record and think that's it, you never appreciate how it affects people," Valentine said afterwards.

Michael J. Grayson, Manager of the-then Theatre Royal in the 1970s-80s, placed an advert in The Stage asking if anyone was interested in helping with a benefit in aid of the widow of Frederick De Birch, former House Manager of the Theatre Royal. The Benefit Performance was being held on Sunday January 25th, 1981. Years later another benefit performance was held for Peter Sarah, Manager of the Theatre Royal who had suddenly died in the Theatre Royal. His funeral service had taken place at the Cathedral in Newcastle. I recall asking Michael Grayson about the possibility of any jobs at the Theatre Royal when I left school, he was quite dismissive I remember, but did predict I would no doubt maintain a connection with the Theatre Royal long after he had gone. Also, Peter Sarah supported my setting up a website based on theatre North East.

Stephen Martin remembers he started working on stage as a part-time stagehand in December 1974. His memories of the first Pantomime include the staff, in particular the long serving Stage Manager George Spencer and Ralph on the Stage Door. Drinks in the Adelphi, if a bit flush in the Royal Turks Hotel opposite the Royal and emergency food available, e.g., on Sunday mornings in the Worsick Street Bus Station. Before the last modernisation of the Theatre the old Stage door was next door to a clothes shop owned by a member of the band Geordie which included Brian Johnson, you could hear them rehearse in their basement. Little did we know we were listening to a future AC/ DC front man.

Chris Hayward, who has played Dame in recent years at the Theatre Royal and an integral part of the Theatre Royal pantomimes breaking box office records year after year and being the No 1 panto in the country, remembers thinking he would never play his home town. Chris recalls his career taking him all over the UK, but never Newcastle. Finally Michael Harrison. M.D. of Qdos Pantomimes, had the opportunity to bring Chris "home" but he was already committed to a pantomime elsewhere. However, finally, Chris joined Clive Webb and Danny Adams to be part of the Theatre Royal panto dynasty, who fill the Theatre Royal week on week, year after year. Apart from appearing in panto Chris now dedicates his time to his formal menswear business in the Heaton area of Newcastle.

But Chris is from a theatrical family and can recall stories of previous productions at the Theatre Royal, one being a pantomime in the 1930s. The stage contained two large swimming pools, one hidden from the audience, but linked by a large tube.

Dancers were asked to attend auditions providing the relevant swimming certificates.

The idea was that as the curtain rose there were dancers on stage and in the pool, who appeared to dive in the water and disappear as they never resurfaced from the audiences point of view. In fact they actually swam through the tube and resurfaced backstage, but left the audience puzzled as to where they went. All went well until a swimmer (who was slightly large) became jammed in the tube. This caused the dancer following to have to resurface and continue to dance in the water in front of the audience while the backstage crew sorted the issue out.

Ray Irwin, one of the Stage Doorkeepers at the Theatre Royal, has Billy Clark to thank for him getting the job. He remembers sitting around the Stage Door area waiting for his daughter who was being shown around the stage, during a run of ***Blood Brothers***, when Billy (then Stage Doorkeeper) noticed he was interested in the theatre. Billy told him to contact the Theatre Royal if he ever had an interest in getting a job there. Years later he had to leave working for the Evening Chronicle after thirty two years following an accident. After a brief spell working elsewhere, he contacted the Theatre Royal to ask if there were any vacancies. As it happened there were, but the deadline had just passed. He was advised to write in anyway and out of the blue he was contacted and started as Stage Doorkeeper shortly afterwards. He has now been in his role for ten years and it's a labour of love, because he loves the theatre.

In 1941 Mervyn Rolando, The famous Burlesque Artist, ran an advertisement which stated he wished to thank: "*Mr and Mrs Syd Seymour for the long tour of Mad Hatters - for further contracts and releasing him to play in Emile Littler's Aladdin at the Theatre Royal Newcastle and also for his handsome Christmas Gift.*"

Trish Hayes recalls her Great Uncle being Manager of the Theatre Royal for many years. Freddie Rumball was a flamboyant character by all accounts. He always wore a trademark bow tie and met the audiences in evening dress. Trish recalls being given complimentary seats to see several performances. On other occasions when going to visit her Great Uncle, actually going in to see the productions, while being placed in the care of the usherettes. Freddie Rumball retired from the Theatre Royal in the early 1960s having worked there for over forty years.

I have also been told about a very famous British actress (who is well know for her roles in TV series on both sides of the Atlantic and still appears on TV today) playing the Theatre Royal in a tour of a play, a few years ago. After a visit to a radio station she was being driven back to the Theatre Royal, when she commented on not having enough sockets in her dressing room and requested an extension lead. As there was a Homebase close by, a detour was made. But the actress decided not to stay in the car and walked around the store in Kingston Park. Shoppers took a double take, as they tried to work out if it was a look alike or understand why a world famous actress was wandering round their local Homebase.

The Front of House staff have to deal with customer queries at every performance, but often the questions seem rather strange, but as they say, no question is daft if you do not know the answer!

Question (on a Thursday afternoon, when the audience is significantly older): *Have you seen my husband go in to the Stall, he has grey hair and glasses?*
Answer: *Sorry, that accounts for ninety five percent of the men in there, madam.*

Question: *Do you know if my husband has gone to his seat already?*
Answer: *Sorry I do not know your husband!*

Question: *Does this lift just go all the way up?*
Answer: *No, and back down, sir*

Memories from the Audience

Originally I was going to start this project from the 1950's, but when several people contacted me with memories from productions playing the Theatre from the mid 1930's, I thought we should start from there.

Mrs. Pearson of Whitley Bay recalls:

"We were always disappointed if we were unable to get a seat in the front of the Gallery, to avoid the brass rail." If the Carl Rosa were performing she would go three times a week as the train journey from Whitley Bay was reduced after 5 p.m. to one shilling. Her earliest memory was of attending ***Die Fledermaus***, with her then boyfriend, who she later married and I must thank Mrs. Pearson for donating her large collection of programmes from this era to assist me with this Memories project.

So I thought we should digress briefly and take a look at the programmes from the 1930s and 40s as they are very different from today's style.

In October 1936 Lilac Time played the Royal when the Manager was William Whitehead and the Assistant Manager was the aforementioned Fred Rumball. Prices were: Stalls: 6 shillings, 4 shillings and 9 pence. Grand Circle: 5 shillings. Pit Stalls: 3

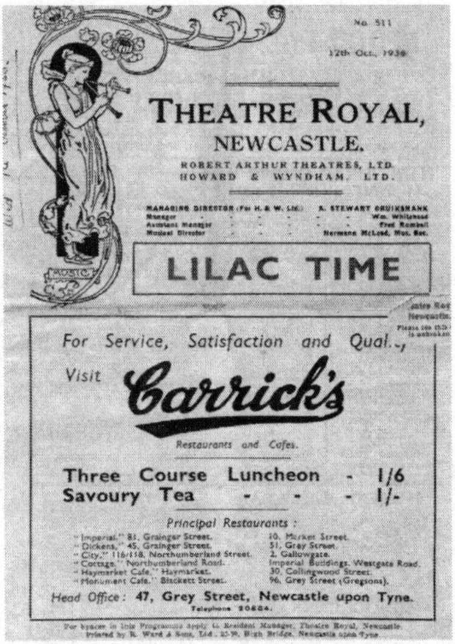

shillings and sixpence. Upper Circle: 3 Shillings and 2 Shillings and sixpence. Amphitheatre: 1 Shilling and sixpence. Gallery: 1 Shilling. But matinees were cheaper! An advert for Carrick's shared the front page. But, when reading the programme for this production there is a note stating:

"The Management will esteem it a favour if all Ladies would remove their hats, as it is obvious that the enjoyment of many is entirely spoilt, owning to their view being obstructed by it."

The programmes were sealed with a wrap around tab which had to be broken to read it and mainly contained adverts, some of the names are still familiar today, even if no longer in business:

F Robson & Co Opticians of Pilgrim Street and Dean Street
Universal Building Society with Mortgages at 4.5%
Pumphrey's Coffee of The Cloth Market
Risi's Ices

Later in the decade the programmes changed to a slightly more substantial booklet, still sealed but under the name Theatre Royal, Newcastle, Messrs. Robert Arthur Theatres Co. Limited and Messrs. Howard and Wyndham, Limited, were listed. The front cover shows the Theatre Royal at night with cars parked outside and people walking by the portico.

While the adverts remained generally the same, all be it Moses had no sale on the fur coats, the florist advertised is Mrs. I Gaskin of Grainger Arcade. Today we recognise the name Sarah Gaskin in relation to flowers, not Mrs. I.

The Theatre Royal played host to ***The Original Ice Theatre Spectacle*** as seen and approved by over a million people at the London Coliseum according to the programmes. The three act ***"St. Moritz"*** played a short season from May 2nd 1938 and promised revelry, laughter, music and spectacle.

The cast included Bianca Schenk: English and Austrian Gold Medallist, who had also competed in the Olympics and became runner up in the Austrian Championship. As well as many other top skaters and Rene Rougemont ***The Stilt Skater*** and Starita, ***The Skating Soubrette*** in the very large cast.

In the advertisements John Moses of Grainger Street was now advertising: ***Leichner Hormone Cream***, which promised to make New Tissues grow so that tiny lines would disappear and only appear in the gaiety of laughter. A 12/6 Shilling jar was meant to last for four months.

However, the front of the programme, above the title of the production, contained a reminder:
'Physicians and others with booked seats, who anticipate being summoned during the Performance, are requested to acquaint the Box office with the number of their seats."

Also the Box office was open 10 a.m. until 9 p.m. with bookings open only two weeks before the performance, but the Station Hotel had a private telephone line direct to the Box Office.

Productions which played the Theatre Royal during the late 1930's, included ***The Corn is Green*** starring Sybil Thorndyke, ***Under Your Hat*** starring Jack Hulbert and Cicely Courtneidge, Donald Wolfit starring for a week in a different Shakespeare play each day, on the Saturday Matinees it was **The *Merchant of Venice***, while the evening saw him perform in ***Macbeth***.

In the autumn of 1939 "***Spring Time for Henry***" starred Michael Redgrave, Roger Livesey and Rachel Kempson.

The programmes now carried an announcement asking patrons to note the following:
"All Attendants in this theatre wear a special numbered badge. If a patron wishes to recognise good service, the number of the badge will distinguish the Attendant concerned."

Returning to people memories **Mrs. I of Fenham** is 89 years old and remembers in the 30's and 40's buskers entertaining the waiting queues as she queued up for the Gallery, one she particularly remembered was a man who made items from paper, especially ladders. She used to pay one shilling to a lady behind a grille when the Gallery entrance opened and although the Amphitheatre had padding on the seats, and cost slightly more, she liked to sit in the Gallery as it had slightly more leg room, even though it was really just wooden steps. She recalls a Commissionaire telling people to move along, no one ever argued, they just moved to make more room. But when his back was turned they all shuffled back again.

Mrs. H. from North Shields recalls:
"We, (my Uncle Tom, brother Ken and myself) attended the pantomime every year from 1931 until 1938. Uncle Tom then emigrated to Australia just before World War Two in 1939."

Added to the programmes during this time was the following warning:

Theatre Royal - Newcastle-on-Tyne

ROBERT ARTHUR THEATRES CO., LTD. HOWARD & WYNDHAM, LTD.
Managing Director (H. & W., Ltd.) - A. STEWART CRUIKSHANK
Manager - WILLIAM WHITEHEAD
Assistant Manager - FRED KIMBALL
Musical Adviser - HERMANN McLEOD, Mus.Bac.

BOX OFFICE OPEN DAILY AT THEATRE. 'Phone, N'cle 22061.
Station Hotel private line direct to Box Office.
Box Plans open Two Weeks ahead for all Attractions.
The Management reserve the right to refuse admission.

N.B.—All Attendants in this theatre wear a special numbered badge. If a patron wishes to recognise good service, the number of the badge will distinguish the Attendant concerned.

N.B.—PHYSICIANS and others with booked seats, who anticipate being summoned during the Performance are requested to acquaint the Box Office with the number of their seats.

AIR RAIDS: You will be notified by the manager if warning is given, do not be alarmed, because the warning does not mean that a Raid will take place, and it is not likely to occur for at least five minutes. If you wish to leave for home or shelter near at hand you are at liberty to leave the theatre. If not you should remain in the building, which is much safer than on the streets. Keep calm, it may not happen. The performance will continue.

Commencing TUESDAY, NOVEMBER 12th, 1940. For TWO WEEKS.
MATINEES DAILY (EXCEPT MONDAYS) AT 2.
Each WEDNESDAY and SATURDAY EVENING at 6 p.m.

"AIR RAIDS: You will be notified by the manager if warning is given, do not be alarmed, because the warning does not mean that a Raid will take place, and it is not likely to take place for at least five minutes. If you wish to leave for home or shelter near at hand you are at liberty to leave the theatre, if not you should remain in the building, which is much safer than on the streets. Keep calm, it may not happen. The performance will continue."

Also the following advert started to appear:

"ENTERTAINMENT IS ESSENTIAL: Let us preserve our balance. ENTERTAINMENT IS AN ESSENTIAL WAR INDUSTRY. It gives a much-needed relief to strained nerves and tired minds. It gives relaxation to the fighting men on leave."

Early in the decade, March 1940, a play called "***Jupiter Laughs***", played the Theatre and in the cast was a young actor called James Mason playing a

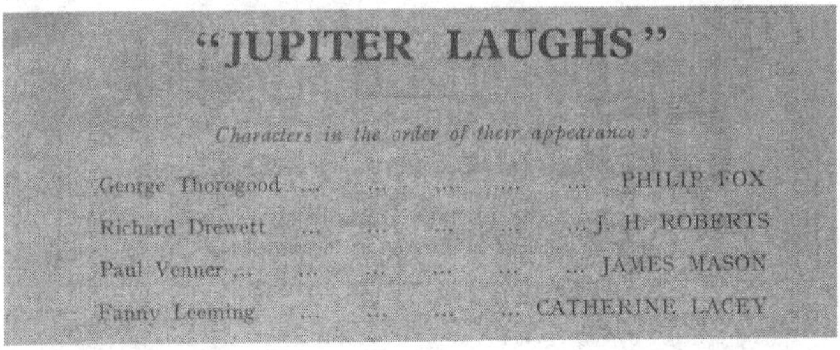
"JUPITER LAUGHS"

Characters in the order of their appearance:

George Thorogood	PHILIP FOX
Richard Drewett	J. H. ROBERTS
Paul Venner	JAMES MASON
Fanny Leeming	CATHERINE LACEY

character called Paul Venner. The whole action took place in a doctor's common room at Hopewell Towers. Mason went on to international stardom of course. But it is always interesting to catch sight of a name, often in the chorus, who later becomes a household name like Sean Connery, who has played the Theatre Royal on more than one occasion.

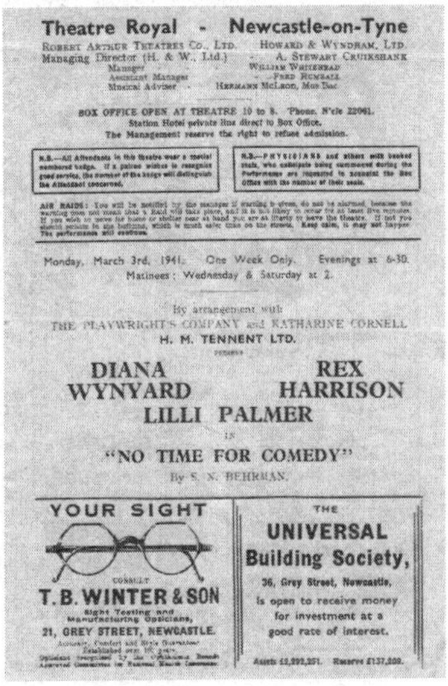
Theatre Royal - Newcastle-on-Tyne

Robert Arthur Theatres Co., Ltd. Howard & Wyndham, Ltd.
Managing Director (H. & W., Ltd.) - A. Stewart Cruikshank
Manager - - William Whitehead
Assistant Manager - - Fred Humball
Musical Adviser - Hermann McLeod, Mus.Bac.

BOX OFFICE OPEN AT THEATRE 10 to 8. 'Phone, N'cle 22061.
Station Hotel private line direct to Box Office.
The Management reserve the right to refuse admission.

N.B.—All Attendants in this theatre wear a special numbered badge. If a patron wishes to recognise good service, the number of the badge will distinguish the Attendant concerned.

N.B.—PHYSICIANS and others with booked seats, who anticipate being summoned during the Performance are requested to acquaint the Box Office with the number of their seats.

AIR RAIDS: You will be notified by the manager if warning is given, do not be alarmed, because the warning does not mean that a Raid will take place, and it is not likely to occur for at least five minutes. If you wish to leave for home or shelter near at hand you are at liberty to leave the theatre. If not you should remain in the building, which is much safer than on the streets. Keep calm, it may not happen. The performance will continue.

Monday, March 3rd, 1941. One Week Only. Evenings at 6-30.
Matinees: Wednesday & Saturday at 2.

By arrangement with
THE PLAYWRIGHTS COMPANY and KATHARINE CORNELL
H. M. TENNENT LTD.
presents

DIANA WYNYARD REX HARRISON
LILLI PALMER
in
"NO TIME FOR COMEDY"
By S. N. BEHRMAN.

YOUR SIGHT
consult
T.B. WINTER & SON
Sight Testing and Manufacturing Opticians,
21, GREY STREET, NEWCASTLE.

THE
UNIVERSAL
Building Society,
36, Grey Street, Newcastle,
is open to receive money for investment at a good rate of interest.
Assets £2,292,351. Reserve £137,200.

No Time For Comedy played in 1941, brought Rex Harrison and Lilli Palmer to the Theatre and we will hear more about Rex Harrison later. But the programme clearly shows the warning notes regarding air raids, doctors and recommending Theatre Royal Staff.

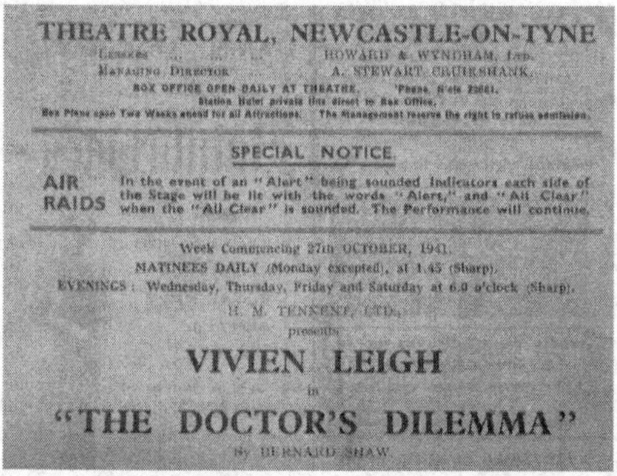

THEATRE ROYAL, NEWCASTLE-ON-TYNE

LESSEES ... ... HOWARD & WYNDHAM, LTD.

MANAGING DIRECTOR ... A. STEWART CRUIKSHANK.

BOX OFFICE OPEN DAILY AT THEATRE. 'Phone, N'cle 22001.

Station Hotel private line direct to Box Office.

Box Plans open Two Weeks ahead for all Attractions. The Management reserve the right to refuse admission.

SPECIAL NOTICE

AIR RAIDS In the event of an "Alert" being sounded Indicators each side of the Stage will be lit with the words "Alert," and "All Clear" when the "All Clear" is sounded. The Performance will continue.

Week Commencing 27th OCTOBER, 1941.

MATINEES DAILY (Monday excepted), at 1.45 (Sharp).

EVENINGS: Wednesday, Thursday, Friday and Saturday at 6.0 o'clock (Sharp).

H. M. TENNENT, LTD.,

presents

VIVIEN LEIGH

in

"THE DOCTOR'S DILEMMA"

by BERNARD SHAW

By 1941 the programmes had retuned to a more flimsy design and **Vivien Leigh** was gracing the Theatre Royal stage in Bernard Shaw's ***The Doctor's Dilemma.*** This is just one of several appearances Vivien Leigh made at the Theatre Royal.

The Air Raid warning was changed to the following:

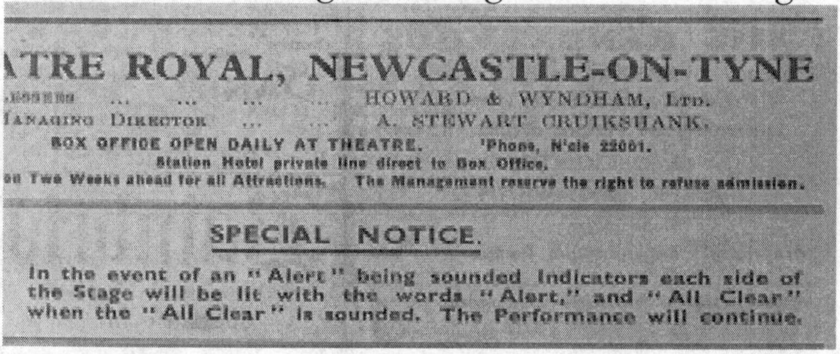

TRE ROYAL, NEWCASTLE-ON-TYNE

ESSEES ... ... HOWARD & WYNDHAM, LTD.

ANAGING DIRECTOR ... A. STEWART CRUIKSHANK.

BOX OFFICE OPEN DAILY AT THEATRE. 'Phone, N'cle 22001.

Station Hotel private line direct to Box Office.

en Two Weeks ahead for all Attractions. The Management reserve the right to refuse admission.

SPECIAL NOTICE.

In the event of an "Alert" being sounded Indicators each side of the Stage will be lit with the words "Alert," and "All Clear" when the "All Clear" is sounded. The Performance will continue.

"In the event of an 'Alert' being sounded indicators each side of the Stage will be lit with the words 'Alert' and 'All Clear' when the 'All Clear' is sounded. The Performance will continue."

Also listed in the programme were details of the Theatre Royal Piano String Quartet and adverts for

Bainbridge & Co, specialising in uniforms and outfits for Officers in the Royal Navy, Army and R.A.F., started to appear alongside other company names that became instantly recognisable for some time, some of which are still around today:
Stan Seymour, equipment for all sports
Alderson and Brentnall for pianos
Isaac Walton's for uniforms
J.G. Windows of the Central Arcade for everything in music, radio and records.

During the rest of the 1940's the programmes changed to a simple folded white design, which upon opening had to be folded out and turned around to read. The central panel contained all the show details, cast and character names, details of each Act, etc. While all around this panel were plain adverts. The Box Office now closed at 8 p.m. rather than 9 p.m.

Artistes who appeared during this time included: ***Margot Fonteyn, Moria Shearer, Max Wall,***

Michael Redgrave, Evelyn Laye, Robertson Hare, Constance Cummings, Ian Fleming, Wilfred Pickles, June Whitfield and Flora Robson.

Mrs. B from West Denton recalls when she was a teenager in the 1940's and, going to her seat in the Gods, dropped her gas mask, which was in a round tin. The gas mask proceeded to bounce down the steps of the Gods, from the back to the front row. She was very embarrassed.

Mrs. S of Newcastle recalls:
"In the early days of World War Two, my dad was a butcher and because of rationing, people offered all sorts of bribes to get an extra bit of sausage, black pudding or whatever they could in with their rations. One of his customers was a cheeky chap called Tommy, who was an usher at the Theatre Royal. Dad used to get regular tickets for the Theatre from him and I recall being taken to see Peter Pan with Celia Lipton, in what seems to be a million years ago. This production whetted my appetite for more Peter Pans and over the years I have seen "Peter" played by Margaret Lockwood, with her daughter

Julia playing Wendy. In a later production Julia played Peter, as did Phyllis Calvert. Captain Hook was played by the likes of Alastair Sims and Victor Spinetti. In later years I took my own children to see Peter Pan, when Anita Harris played "Peter" before the most memorable performance of them all, Bonnie Langford as the high flying Peter.

Once the War ended, so did the bribes and we started to attend productions by sitting in the Gods. I remember being urged to move along to create more room, but the audience used to bob up and down, giving the illusion of moving along, but actually we stayed exactly where we were.

The heat in the Gods was overwhelming but one occasion, when watching South Pacific the temperature added to the authenticity of the piece!

Of the plays I saw from the Gods Othello starring Orson Wells with Gudrun Ure (who much later became Super Gran) as Desdemona and Arsenic and Old lace, with Sybil Thorndike, stay firmly in my mind. While one of the worst productions was with a cast of big T.V. names, which was so dire, I refuse to name them. I still attend the Theatre Royal from time to time, but can no longer attempt the climb to the Gods.

Mrs S of Gosforth recalls:

'While having many happy memories of visiting the Theatre Royal, especially during the War, April 6th 1944 is the most memorable. It was my brother's 21st birthday and he had managed to get a 48-hour pass from the R.A.F., where he worked as a Wireless Operator. He caught a train from the South to Newcastle and met our parents and me at the

Theatre Royal, where he had a wonderful evening watching Robert Morley and Vera Pearce in 'Staff Dance'."

Mrs. H from Haltwhistle says:

"I remember during the 1940's being around four years of age and frightened of a big green glittering dragon, during the pantomime. My Mother and Aunt had to reassure me that it was not real!"

By the 1950's programmes had returned to a more substantial booklet form, still sealed and costing sixpence.

Mrs Dinning of Gosforth remembers:

"Whenever I visit the Theatre Royal I recall sitting in a Box near the stage to see Dickie Valentine in pantomime. When he asked for someone to join him on stage to sing his then current hit "The Christmas Alphabet", I was handed on to the stage from the box to sing the song with him. I remember thoroughly enjoying the applause and kiss from him."

Paddy MacDee of Radio Newcastle recalls:
"I entered a competition to win tickets to see Dickie Valentine in Pantomime during the 1950's and was convinced I would win. Sure enough I won two tickets and my parents bought an extra seat so we could all attend the show."

Mr. B. Scott of Forest Hall contacted me to say:
'My Dad landed a job as a stagehand at the Theatre Royal and we received tickets to see one of the productions. I assume they were complimentary as we would not have been able to afford such a grand night out.

I asked my Dad, as any small child would 'Will you be on stage Dad?' In a very matter a fact way, but just enough to appease a young child, he replied 'What I'll do is stick my feet out from under the side curtains so you will know it's me'.

I can remember the colour, grandeur and buzz of excitement all around, until the overture began and we heard "Oh What A Beautiful Morning" from Oklahoma. As the curtain rose, two or three people were standing around a five bar gate, singing their hearts out. But what was so special, that, right on cue, my Dad stuck his brown shoes out from under the side curtain as promised. My Dad was now a star who had appeared on stage at the famous Theatre Royal."

"My husband and I were sitting in our seats waiting for the show to start," recalls **Mrs. S of Chapel House, Newcastle,** *"when a couple arrived, the lady stating most indignantly that we were occupying their seats. Even though we showed her our tickets for that performance, an usherette was summoned. Her husband stood quietly by while this unfolded. Upon inspection they were told their tickets were for the previous evening, no apology was made as they made their hurried exit."*

Of the 1960's Mr. Vout of Gosforth recalls: *"Around 1962 Jimmy Logan was appearing in pantomime and our two boys had recently had their tonsils removed. So I said I would write to Jimmy Logan to ask if we could meet him after the show.*

Permission was granted; Jimmy was so kind, having a long chat with us all (my two boys, daughter, my wife and I). There was no rush involved and we came away delighted to have seen the show and to have met the star in person."

Mr. Elliott of Byker tells us:

"In the early 1960's I made my first visit to the Theatre Royal to see a pantomime starring Jimmy Clitheroe, Jimmy Logan and I believe Mollie Sugden. At the time we lived in Houghton Le Spring and only came to Newcastle on special occasions, as it was an hour on the bus.

When we arrived at Worsick Street Bus Station we walked to Fenwick's for a meal before going to the Theatre Royal. Dad collected the tickets from the Foyer and we bought sweets from the shop, before taking our seats in the front stalls. I, like my parents, elder brother and sister, was an avid listener to the Jimmy Clitheroe Show on the radio every Sunday afternoon. I recall being mesmerised by the inside of the Theatre Royal and thought it was very dramatic when the lights went out and performers came on to the stage. Apparently I never stopped talking about the pantomime for weeks!"

Being heavily pregnant did not stop **Mrs. G from Cramlington** attending a performance of Oliver! in the Gallery!:

"In 1967 we went to see Oliver! From the Gallery! Being heavily pregnant we were not sure we should go, but had an overnight bag in the car parked outside, just in case! Not long after I gave birth to my daughter who is now in her mid 40's and we can take her children with us to the Theatre Royal."

David Littlefield was cast as a child actor in the early 1960's when the Newcastle Amateur Operatic Society played the Theatre Royal, performing The Gondoliers and The Mikado on alternate nights.

He remembers being a drummer boy in The Gondoliers and carrying KoKo's axe in the Mikado. To this day he remembers the distinct heady mixture of make-up, paint and scenery and just loved it.

When the men's chorus invited him for a drink he felt very grown up and the "Theatre Bug" was well and truly caught. This led to him joining the queue for "the Gods".

He recalls Adam Faith appearing in Emlyn Williams' play "Night Must Fall" around 1965 chatting to the people in the queue. But best of all on his way to join the queue for the Gods an elderly couple asked for help on crossing Grey Street. It was only when he was half way across he realised on one arm he had Dame Sybil Thorndike and on the other, her husband Lewis Casson, both, he recalls, were extremely charming.

Stairway to The Gods

Mrs. P. Tomlinson can recall:

"About 60 years ago, when I was quite young, my parents would take my sister and I to two or sometimes three (if we were very good) pantomimes. Even at that young age I always

remember the Theatre Royal was by far the best with its lavish costumes and scenery. My next memory was when I was at Whitley Bay Grammar School and one of my friends suggested we went to the theatre.

We were in the front row of 'the Gods' and saw 'Call me Madam'. As we leaned over the edge, I was absolutely entranced and this started my love affair with the theatre and particularly in musicals. It wasn't until many years later when I reluctantly threw away my vast collection of 4d programmes that I realised that taking the lead was Noelle Gordon (Meg Richardson in Crossroads). After that we went every week (regardless of what was on) straight from school, standing in the queue, feeling quite grownup, reading the latest magazine, Cosmopolitan. Then when the door was open, we would run up the staircase to 'the Gods' where we were packed in like sardines - no seats in those days!

When I left school and started work, I continued to go every week and book for the following week. Gradually other things took over my life and I only went when there was something special I wanted to see.

Fourteen years ago I retired and started going much more, became a Friend of the Theatre Royal and even have my seat - where? In the Gods of course!"

Philip Walton of Gosforth recalls:

'I have a lifetime of wonderful memories of performances at the Theatre Royal. As a child my parents took me to pantomime, musicals and operetta- shows such as The Desert Song, The New Moon, Lilac Time, and Balalaika etc., that sadly we rarely hear these days!

I quickly moved up the ladder to the "old" D'Oyly Carte in their "silver age" and on to regular visits by Sadler's Wells Opera (now English National) and a succession of wonderful productions - no "concept" productions then! I particularly recall a wonderful production of The Flying Dutchman (in its three act edition) by Dennis Arundell with excellent designs by Timothy O'Brien and superb lighting by Charles Bristow - the appearance of the ghostly ship in Act 1 drew gasps from the audience! The Wells gave us a wide repertoire including operetta as it should be done! The Royal Ballet Touring Company were also a vital date in my diary and their opening night performances with Doreen Wells and David Wall will always remain in my memory as truly outstanding nights in the theatre. When the Company gave a three week season in the spring of 1969 I was fortunate to be able to attend twenty-one of the twenty-four performances!

After Sir Kenneth MacMillan joined the two Royal Ballet companies together we had a visit in 1971 by the Covent Garden company from which I remember a wonderful Swan Lake with Antoinette Sibley and Anthony Dowell and a few nights later the cast was led by Dame Margot Fonteyn superbly partnered, (as always) by David Wall.

In the early 1970s we were treated to a wonderful Sunday evening recital given by Dame Elisabeth Schwarzkopf as part of the short-lived Newcastle Festival , and then all those

wonderful evenings of Scottish Opera in their heyday before the Scottish Executive pulled the rug from under their feet!! - great evenings of Strauss, Verdi, Wagner including the one hundredth performance as Hans Sachs by Norman Bailey - I was at Covent Garden on the memorable night he sang his first Hans Sachs in that house taking over from Hubert Hofmann at just seven hours notice to save the opening night of a new production – after that performance he was invited to sing the role at Bayreuth and his international career took off! I could go on forever!!!

Finally I remember queuing for long hours for the gallery followed by the wild dash upstairs to get the best seats in the days when the gallery was a gallery!!!!

I look forward to the completion of the refurbishment of the theatre and to many more great performances!"

Mr. Birch of Gosforth remembers:

'Whenever I could I would take my friends to the Theatre and to be fair a group of us often attended on a Saturday evening, ok slightly out of the ordinary for a group of guys in their early 20's but we enjoyed

it, sometimes! I can recall around five of us were watching STEAMING, a comedy set in a Turkish bath, which had won may awards, but contained a lot of female nudity, including Anna Karen (Olive from On The Buses I seem to recall). At the interval the lady in front turned round and asked us why we had come to the show, as she could not understand so many people (the Theatre Royal was very full) coming to see this production. The reason for her questioning turned out to be that the week previously she had attended when a P.G. Woodhouse play was on and the Theatre had been almost empty and she failed to understand why. We stumbled over our answers, stating it was because it was an award winning comedy etc., and did not have the guts to tell her the billing of female nudity had almost certainly had a lot to do with attracting a large audience."

"Anton Petrov used to play the piano in the orchestra pit in the 1980s. Years before," recalls **Mr. White of Pelaw**, *"he was a well-known band leader in the area. At the end of the interval, you could see his hand appear over the front rail of the pit and wave in appreciation to the applause before the curtain rose once again. We always used to shout for more, after sitting through his repertoire of songs from the shows. Tragically he died after a break in at his home."*

Mrs. Archer of North Tyneside recalls: *"In the 1980s we went to see TV stars of the day Jill Gascoine (Cats Eyes) and Bryan Marshall (Warship). They were the only ones in the play set in a chalet up a mountain, I seem to recall. Suddenly there were shouts for an unlisted person called Mary and the curtain was dropped. Then we were asked 'Is there a doctor in the house" and there was! Mr. Marshall had taken* *ill and when he collapsed we had assumed it was part of the plot. The rest of the show was cancelled and once he was checked out the show ran for the rest of the week and we had to sit through it again. But really once had been enough and we had worked out the end already, but duly returned".*

Mr. White of Ponteland remembers:
'We saw Christopher Cazenove and a girl who was very well known at the time for being in the Renault TV adverts as Nicole. The play was advertised as having nudity, which meant more bums on seats. But when the time came for the young lady to strip off a camera flashed and Mr. Cazenove shouted at someone to stop the man with the camera as he fled the stalls."

Mr. K. Proctor of Ashington has many memories of visiting the Theatre Royal. But one of his favourites is Dad's Army, which contained most of the original TV cast, but our own "Wacky Jacky" Jack Haig played Corporal Jones. He recalls this being a wonderful show with news- reels showing in the background and perfect entertainment. As well as Julie Rogers showing off her wonderful pair of legs in the pantomime Jack and the Beanstalk. While he also spotted Charlton Heston across the street, when he reopened the Theatre Royal in the 1980s in a production of A Man for All Seasons. He was with his late brother at the time, but neither could go over to speak to what he considers to be possibly the biggest film star to appear at the Theatre Royal.

Mr. Richards of Byker recalls:
"When the RSC production of Nicholas Nickleby was at the Theatre, you had to go over two nights. Before one of the evenings a group of friends and I went to the Rupali restaurant in the Bigg Market, where the owner, Mr. Latif (Lord Harpole) was in charge. He was quite a character and well known in the area. For some reason we were running late and had to make a dash across to the Theatre, where we found one of our group starting to pass out poppadum's, (which he had brought with him from the Rupali) to the elderly ladies next to him. They had never experienced Indian food before and we wondered if he had converted them to a new culinary experience, alas we never found out."

But Mrs. Crawford had a different encounter during a one-man play: *"When Donald Sinden was touring in his one-man play about Oscar Wilde, it was extremely hot. Sitting behind us in the Grand Circle was a lady with a very large amount of bangles running up her arm; every time she moved so did the bangles. If the show had been a musical there would not have been an issue but in a one-man play it was very annoying. We found the lady sitting next to*

us glaring over believing we were making the noise and had to try and let her know it was coming from behind us, but she appeared to be getting more and more annoyed, which, on top of the sound of the bangles, was spoiling the evening for us. So at the interval, I apologised and pointed out it was not us, then turned to the lady behind and asked if she could stop the bangles from clashing. Regretfully she did not take the request in the best way possible and refused to see the problem. I pointed out that it was not just annoying us and turned to the lady next to us for moral support. Suddenly she seemed to have paralysis of the neck, as well as having been struck deaf and dumb. She sat, head fixed looking up towards the ceiling, apparently unable to hear my question about her being annoyed or the bangles spoiling her enjoyment. Miraculously as the lady behind, begrudgingly sorted out the problem and the lights dimmed once more, I noticed she was able to move her head freely once again and could obviously hear what was being said on stage."

Keith Anthony remembers the year 1984:

"The caravanette, wife, two kids and the dog, working our way up the east coast from Leicestershire to visit brother-in-law in Jesmond Dene. Being avid real ale drinkers, with a 1981 copy of Camra's Good Beer Guide we sloped off from Jesmond to hit the Toon. Found the then Royal Buffet to sample the Vaux Sunderland Draught Bitter. Whilst quaffing, noticed Leonard Rossiter embibing. I ventured over with, 'I don't collect autographs, but my wife does: do you mind?' Leonard duly obliged and I went back to my pint. Lovely smile, lovely moment. Hadn't done it before, haven't done it since!!"

"For me personally, one memory always pops in to my mind whenever I see Joanna Lumley on television", **remembers Mr. D. Wells of North Tyneside:** *"Ms. Lumley instantly takes me back to the time she appeared in Private Lives. Before the show opened on the Monday we were aware of a problem, as a slip of paper in the programme informed us the leading actor was not performing and Simon Cadell had taken over as the lead. At the time he was well known for appearing in the hit television comedy Hi De Hi. Before the show started, Joanne Lumley appeared in front of the house curtain and explained that the leading actor in the tour had been taken ill towards the end of the previous week. There was no understudy and rather than cancel the end of the tour Simon Cadell, who had played the part fairly recently, would take over. But the cast had only met him that morning and rehearsed on the train from London, before arriving at the Theatre Royal. However, Simon's costumes had not arrived but they were going ahead with the performance. The next couple of hours were gripping, as not only the play was very good, but the entire audience was willing Simon to get through. I only recall him faltering once, when the prompt had to shout a line from off stage. He was greeted by cheers as he took his curtain call."*

Sue from County Durham fondly remembers being married at the Theatre Royal:
"The service was held in what was then the Monet Room at the top of the original stairs to the Grand Circle. She recalls standing in the quietness of the magnificent room, knowing just outside life was going on at its normal fast pace. They did invite

John Challis and Sue Holderness (Boycie and Marlene from Only Fools and Horses) to join them as they were appearing at the Theatre Royal that week, regrettably, due to other commitments, they could not."

Gail Treliving tells us that she experienced the most embarrassing moment of her life at the Theatre Royal.:

"It was back in the late 1990s/early 2000s (I can't exactly remember when) and my husband and I were there to watch a RSC production. At the time there was a cartoon satire show on ITV called (I think) 2DTV, which I used to watch but which my husband didn't. While we were waiting for the play to begin, I was telling him about the previous night's show, in which the North East MP, John Cunningham (in the cabinet at the time) had been portrayed as a Geordie 'hard man' who kept threatening to put 'a nut' on anyone who disagreed with him. I was re-enacting the sketch, along with suitable head movements and imitating his accent when suddenly my husband saw a head looming round on my right, belonging to - JOHN CUNNINGHAM! We were totally unaware that he had been sitting right beside me. I wanted the earth to open up and swallow me when I realised he must have overheard me but he was awfully nice about it, and I'm certainly glad I hadn't said anything derogatory. So - the moral of the story is, always check who you're sitting beside at the Theatre Royal before opening your mouth!"

Sheila Chandlert of Wallsend recalls:

"Having enjoyed many shows at the Theatre Royal our visit to see Whistle Down the Wind on June 1st 2010 was extremely memorable. On the way to meet my daughter and

granddaughter I fell, but not wanting to disappoint anyone, I limped to the bus, only to collapse as we arrived in Newcastle. So instead of sitting in the Theatre Royal, I was taken by Ambulance to the A&E where a fracture to my big toe was diagnosed. When my daughter rang the Theatre Royal and explained what had happened they were sympathetic and changed our tickets for a performance on Saturday and we even managed to meet "Jesus" afterwards (Jonathon Ansell)."

To finish, for the time being…

Hopefully, this collection of memories has started people reflecting on their own visits to the Theatre Royal. But at the same time it will have no doubt shocked a few people as to how long ago it was since they saw a particular production. Time just marches on.

But, in fact it is not really finished, it never will be; as long as productions play the Theatre Royal there will be memories and I therefore hope this project will result in more people contacting me so we can keep adding to the Theatre Royal Memories.

Therefore, I will be launching www.theatreroyalmemories.co.uk. A dedicated website for this project which will contain all the information in the book as well as new memories.

Please send any new stories to me via the email address: *theatrememories@btinternet.com*

Past Productions

A glance back at shows through my lifetime at the Theatre Royal

To try and list all of the productions which have appeared at the Theatre Royal would be virtually impossible, with Sunday concerts, one-off performances etc., you would almost certainly leave out someone's favourite. It would also be fairly boring to read.

So below is a selection, which includes many stars no longer with us and identifying some productions which just keep returning, with new casts.

The 1960's

Peter Pan starring Julia Lockwood (daughter of Margaret).

It's In The Bag with Terry Thomas.

And Another Thing starring both Lionel and Joyce Blair.

The Bride Comes Back starring Cicely Courtneidge and Robertson Hare.

The Bargain and **Peter Pan** with Alastair Sim.

Waiting In The Wings with Sybil Thorndike.

Time And Yellow Roses and **Close Quarters** with Flora Robson.

August for the People starred Rex Harrison and Rachel Roberts.

The Lizard On The Rock starred Harry Andrews, Sian Phillips and John Laurie.

Breaking Point and **Goodbye Charlie** with John Gregson.

Rattle Of A Simple Man starred Sheila Hancock and Edward Woodward.

The Ides Of March stared John Gielgud.

Uncle Vanya starring Laurence Olivier, Joan Plowright and Frank Finlay.

The Black And White Minstrel Show.

My Fair Lady starred Tony Britton (he would return to the Theatre Royal with Anna Neagle in another version of this musical as we have already discussed).

La Contessa with Vivien Leigh.

Strike A Light starred Evelyn Laye.

Wait Until Dark cast headed by Honour Blackman and Peter Sallis.

On Approval starred Michael Denison and Dulcie Gray.

Relatively Speaking with Celia Johnson, Michael Hordern and Richard Briers.

Getting Married with Ian Carmichael and Moira Lister.

Dear Octopus starring Cicely Courtneidge, Jack Hulbert and Richard Todd.

All For Mary starred Kathleen Harrison.

Night Must Fall with Sybil Thorndike and Adam Faith.

The Man Most Likely To with Leslie Phillips.

Let Sleeping Wives Lie with Brian Rix.

Highly Confidential with Hermione Gingold.

Birds On The Wing with Bruce Forsyth.

On The Rocks starred David Tomlinson, Jack Hulbert and Robert Flemyng.

Little Jack with Harry H. Corbett.

A Woman Named Anne starred Moira Lister.

I've Seen You Cut Lemons starred Diane Cilento and Robert Hardy with Sean Connery directing.

Christmas Shows included:

GOLDILOCKS AND THE THREE BEARS

TOM THUMB Jimmy Clitheroe and Nat Jackley

THE FOL DE ROLS CHRISTMAS PARTY

CINDERELLA Terry Scott, Jimmy Logan, Wendy Bowman

The 1970's

The Black And White Minstrel Show

Pat Phoenix in **The Miracle Worker**

The Mating Game with Terry Scott and Nicholas Parsons

Jimmy Logan season of five plays including Second Honeymoon and The Love Match

Treasure Island with Bernard Miles

The Clandestine Marriage starred Michael Denison, Dulcie Gray and Michele Dotrice

Jimmy Edwards and Eric Sykes in **Big Bad Mouse**

Leslie Phillips in **The Man Most Likely To**

Alastair Sim and Stanley Holloway in **Siege**

Glynis Johns starred in **The Marquise**

TV Comedians starring Frank Carson, Duggie Brown and Colin Crompton

Relative Values starred Margaret Lockwood, Patricia Hayes and Joyce Blair

Irene Handl and Pat Kirkwood appeared in **A Chorus Of Murder**

Hay Fever with Dulcie Gray

Mother Adam starred Peter Wyngarde and Hermione Baddeley

Robert Morley in his own play **A Ghost On Tiptoe**

A Funny Thing Happened On The Way To The Forum starred Phil Silvers (TV's Sgt. Bilko)

Crown Matrimonial had a cast led by Phyllis Calvert

Richard Todd in the stage version of his film hit **The Hasty Heart**

Gaslight with Patricia Phoenix and Alan Browning

Breath of Spring starred Cicely Courtneidge and Jack Hulbert

David Tomlinson in **The Turning Point**

There Goes The Bride starred Bernard Cribbins, Peggy Mount and Terence Alexander

Two And Two Make Sex with Patrick Cargill

John Hanson in **Rose Marie**

Barbara Mullen as Miss Marple in **Murder At The Vicarage**

Anita Harris as **Peter Pan**

The Black Mikado with Michael Denison as Pooh Bah

Barbara Windsor in **A Merry Whiff Of Windsor**

Honor Blackman starred in **The Gentle Hook**

Dame Anna Neagle starred in **The Dame Of Sark**

Roger's Last Stand starred Leslie Phillips and Roy Kinnear.

A Month In The Country with Derek Jacobi, Dorothy Tutin, Jane Lapotaire and Timothy West

Boeing Boeing with Richard O'Sullivan, Sally Thomsett and Yootha Joyce

Brian Rix in **A Bit Between The Teeth**

Busybody with Hylda Baker and with Valentine Dyall

All For Mary starred Jack Smethurst and Sally Thomsett

Three Sisters with Janet Suzman

The Husband In Law starred Peggy Mount and Kenneth Williams

Dad's Army with Arthur Lowe, John le Mesurier, Arthur Ridley, Bill Pertwee and Ian Lavender

Anna Neagle in **The First Mrs. Fraser**

John Mills in **Separate Table**

Danny la Rue

Peggy Mount and Hugh Lloyd in **Porter Must Go**

Maggie (musical of J. M. Barrie's 'What Every Woman Knows') with Dame Anna Neagle

Robin Askwith in **Further Confessions Of A Window Cleaner**

TV hit **George And Mildred** with orginal actors Brian Murphy and Yootha Joyce

Pygmalion with Jennifer Wilson, Paul Daneman, Evelyn Laye and Bill Owen

The Circle with Googie Withers and John McCallum

The Monkey Walk starred Lionel Blair

Suite In Two Keys with Margaret Lockwood Robert Flemyng and Phyllis Calvert

Side By Side By Sondheim starred Bill Steel from Tyne Tees Television as the Narrator along with the touring cast including Mark Wynter and Jill Martin

Worms Eye View with Michael Robbins

My Fair Lady starred Tony Britton, Liz Robertson, Peter Bayliss and Dame Anna Neagle

Harry Worth starred **Pardon Me Prime Minister**

The Wild Duck cast included T. P. McKenna and Benjamin Whitrow

Christmas Shows included:

TREASURE ISLAND Bernard Miles

THE WORLD OF JAMIE –Jimmy Logan

MOTHER GOOSE - Stanley Baxter, Bernard Bresslaw and Mark Wynter

CINDERELLA - Hugh Lloyd, Bill Simpson and George Chisholm

ROBINSON CRUSOE -Mike and Bernie Winters

JACK AND THE BEANSTALK – George Lacy, Jack Douglas, Julie Rogers and Leah Bell

DICK WHITTINGTON Norman Vaughan and Jimmy Thompson

CINDERELLA – David Jason, Bobby Thompson, Leah Bell and Sylvester McCoy

The 1980's

Whose Life Is It Anyway starred Simon Ward

Once a Catholic

Cure for Love starred Christopher Timothy, Carol Drinkwater, Maggie Jones and Dora Bryan

And A Nightingale Sang with Kevin Whately, Madeleine Newton and Stephen Hancock

Peggy Ashcroft in **Watch On The Rhine**
Early Days starred Sir Ralph Richardson

The Caine Mutiny Court Martial cast was headed by Iain Cuthbertson

Private Lives with Joanna Lumley, Simon Cadell joining the cast at very short notice

The Gentle Trap starred Jill Gascoigne and Bryan Marshall

Black Coffee with Hercule Poirot being played by Patrick Cargill

Not Now Darling cast headed by Bernard Cribbins and Derren Nesbitt

The Dresser starred Joss Ackland, Kenneth Haigh and Doreen Mantle

The Wizard Of Oz with Charlie Drake and Meg Johnson

Leonard Rossiter in **The Rules Of The Game** directed by Anthony Quayle

They're Playing Our Song cast was headed by Simon Williams and Sheila White

Fiona Richmond in **Space In My Pyjamas**

Conduct Unbecoming cast included Nyree Dawn Porter and Anthony Steel

Peter O'Toole in **Man And Superman**

A Coat Of Varnish starred Anthony Quayle, Peter Barkworth, John Barron and Carmen Silvera

Irene Handl starred as Mrs. Malaprop in **The Rivals**

Hobson's Choice starred Peter Vaughan, Stephanie Turner and Trevor Bannister

84 Charing Cross Road with Miriam Karlin and Michael Craig

Oliver! cast headed by Roy Hudd and Jimmy Edwards

The Voices with Peter Adamson and Derren Nesbitt

No No Nanette starred Moira Lister replacing Noelle Gordon

Peter Bowles in **Some Of My Best Friends Are Husbands**

The Pack Of Lies cast included Miriam Karlin and George Sewell

Jasper Carrott headed **The Nerd Tour**

When We Are Married with Patrick Cargill, William Lucas, Maria Charles, Avril Angers, Jennifer Wilson, Patsy Rowlands and Jane Freeman

Compo Plays Cupid starred Bill Owen from the TV show Last of The Summer Wine

The Real Thing starred Christopher Timothy and Paula Wilcox

Dennis Waterman and Rula Lenska in **Same Time Next Year**

Saint Joan starred Jane Lapotaire, Tony Britton and Anthony Quayle

Royal Shakespeare Company's **Nicholas Nickleby** (6 weeks run)

Peter Pan The Musical starred Bonnie Langford with Victor Spinetti as Captain Hook

Charlton Heston and Roy Kinnear in **A Man For All Seasons**

The Government Inspector with Anthony Quayle

Rowan Atkinson in **The Sneeze**

Colin Baker revived his TV role to appear in **Dr Who**

Evita with Jacqui Scott and Christopher Corcoran
Veteran's Day starred Jack Lemmon, Michael Gambon and Robert Flemyng

Look Back In Anger directed by Dame Judi Dench starred Kenneth Branagh and Emma Thompson

Beyond Reasonable Doubt with original West End stars Frank Finlay and Wendy Craig as the leads

Christmas Shows included:

JACK AND THE BEANSTALK Barbara Windsor, Spike Rawlings and Ronnie Coyles

DICK WHITTINGTON Ken Goodwin and Tracey Ullman

MOTHER GOOSE Christopher Biggins and Paul Squire

ALADDIN Bernie Winters and Schnorbitz and Anne Aston

.

CINDERELLA The Krankies, Julie Rogers and Charlie Cairoli Junior

SNOW WHITE AND THE SEVEN DWARFS Dana, Mike Newman, Chris Corcoran and Ted Robbins

BABES IN THE WOOD Les Dennis, Frankie Desmond, Anne Nolan, The Two Marks, Andrew Wightman.

CINDERELLA Ronnie Corbett and Patsy Rowlands

The 1990's

Lettice And Lovage cast was headed by Rosemary Leach

South Pacific starred Gemma Craven

Stewart Granger headed the cast of **The Circle**, which also included Ian Carmichael

Ronnie Corbett and Carmen Silvera in **the The Dressmaker**

Run For Your Wife starred Les Dawson

Googie Withers and John McCallum starred in **The Cocktail Hour** the cast of which also included their daughter Joanna McCallum and Nicolas Hammond, best know as Friedrich in the iconic movie The Sound of Music.

Time And The Conways starred Joan Plowright as well as Tasmin Olivier and Julie Kate Olivier with Richard Olivier directing.

Chess with Rebecca Storm

Timothy West and Prunella Scales in **A Long Days Journey Into Night**

Donald Pleasance in **The Caretaker**

Guys And Dolls cast included Barbara Windsor and Gareth Hunt

The Sound Of Music starred Liz Robertson, Christopher Cazenove and Robin Nedwell

Derek Jacobi in **Breaking The Code**

My Fair Lady, directed by Simon Callow, starring Edward Fox and Helen Hobson.

An Ideal Husband starred Hannah Gordon, Michael Denison, Dulcie Gray and Martin Shaw

Lost In Yonkers with Maureen Lipman and Rosemary Harris

Talking Heads cast included Gordon Kaye

Ricochet starred Nigel Havers and Keith Barron

Two Into One with Roy Hudd, Kathy Staff and Alfred Marks

Present Laughter with Tom Conti and Jenny Seagrove

Getting Married starred Dorothy Tutin, Tony Britton, Robert Bathhouse, Barbara Murray, Jane How and Moray Watson

Barnum starring Paul Nicholas

Aspects Of Love cast headed by Kathryn Evans and Gary Bond

Relative Values with Susan Hampshire and Margaret Courtenay.

Scrooge with Anthony Newley, Stratford Johns and Barry Howard

Sweeney Todd and Communicating Doors starred Julia McKenzie

Re Joyce with Maureen Lipman as Joyce Grenfell

Me And My Girl starred Andrew O'Connor

Ten week run of **Cats**

Patricia Routledge in **The Rivals**

Shadowlands with Anton Rodgers and Elizabeth Garvie

Copacabana with Michael Praed

A Passionate Woman with Stephanie Cole

The Mysterious Mr. Love starred Paul Nicholas and Susan Penhaligon

A Doll's House starred Janet McTeer and Owen Teal

Sian Phillips was Marlene Dietrich in **Marlene**

An Ideal Husband starred Simon Ward, Carol Drinkwater, Deborah Grant, Barbara Murray and Richard Todd

Hinge and Bracket in **Lettice And Lovage**

Home Truths starred Christopher Cazenove and Estelle Skornik (best known as Nicole in Renault car ads)

42nd Street with Gemma Craven and Jim Smilie

Elton John's Glasses starred Brian Conley

Alarms And Excursions with Felicity Kendal

The Importance Of Being Earnest with Liza Goddard and Dora Bryan

Annie starred Lesley Joseph and Kevin Colson

Christmas Shows included:

ALADDIN The Krankies, Anita Dobson and Bernard Bresslaw

SNOW WHITE AND THE SEVEN DWARFS Linda Lusardi and Stu Francis

DICK WHITTINGTON AND HIS CAT Su Pollard and the Chuckle Brothers

GOLDILOCKS AND THE THREE BEARS Bobby Davro, Charlie Cairoli Junior and Company, Malandra Burrows and Steve Colman.

JACK AND THE BEANSTALK Little and Large, Ian Reddington and Hilary O'Neil

ROBINSON CRUSOE David Essex and Bobby Bennett

PETER PAN Leslie Grantham and Joe Pasquale

CINDERELLA Philip Middlemiss and Sophie